ISBN 978-0-266-95884-0
PIBN 10915707

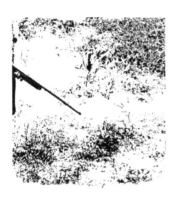

Vol. 18   Nos. 9 & 10
September-October,
1966

Conservation

Pledge

I give my
pledge as an American
to save and faithfully to
defend from waste the
natural resources of
my country—its soil
and minerals, its
forests, waters
and wildlife

*Published Bi-Monthly
in the interest of conservation of Louisiana's natural resources by the
Wild Life and Fisheries
Commission, 400 Royal
Street, New Orleans, Lou-
isiana, 70130.*

LOUISIANA WILD LIFE AND FISHERIES COMMISSION

Subscription Free to Louisiana Residents
Upon Written Request

JOHN J. McKEITHEN
Governor

DR. LESLIE L. GLASGOW
Director

L. S. ST. AMANT   R. K. YANCEY
Asst. Director   *Asst. Director*

LOUISIANA CONSERVATIONIST

STEVE HARMON ....Editor
McFADDEN DUFFY ....Staff Writer
EDNARD WALDO ....Staff Writer
ROBERT DENNIE ....Photographer

*Some bushytails are "foxy" little animals
and it takes lots of hunting "know how"
to bag one of the tricky little rascals.
Some hunters are convinced that all squirrels are ventriloquists. You think you
hear the bark and the ruffle of the tail
up in one tree, then lo and behold he turns
up in the opposite direction. (Photo by
Robert N. Dennie)*

EDITORIAL

L OUISIANA is justifiably envied by many states for its abundance of wildlife and fisheries resources. We are indeed a people blessed beyond measure with outdoor opportunities. Such blessings are not without the responsibilities of trusteeship, however, as we will be judged by posterity on what we waste and what we build as man turns to nature for pleasure and inner peace.

LESLIE L. GLASGOW
Director

The swamps and hills, the woods and fields, the streams and Gulf current have long been my laboratory for work. I view them in the light of not only how they can serve mankind, but also for the knowledge a professional can contribute to make them eternally valuable.

The position of Director of the Louisiana Wildlife and Fisheries Commission, recently bestowed on me by your Commission, is not only a job but a tremendous challenge. It opens a wide door of opportunity to more skillfully employ science and scholarship, combined with wise management and vision, to produce abundant wildlife and fisheries resources for future generations.

Fortunately, I do not accept this challenge empty handed. My entire adult life has been spent working in the field of wildlife and fisheries management, as a research scientist, as a teacher of wildlife management at our state university, and as a hunter and fisherman now concerned primarily with teaching my children a love of the outdoors comparable to that I have enjoyed for a lifetime.

Louisiana now stands at the crossroads, her natural resources and their future resting squarely in the hands of all persons concerned with preservation and perpetuation of these God given assets. The encroachment of an expanding civilization constantly makes demands on the outdoors—demands that cannot be met with counterdemands because of man's progress but must be met, rather, with scientific knowledge and sound principles of management so that both sport and commercial interests, working together, can continue to reap maximum benefits from the harvestable surpluses of these resources.

Louisiana sportsmen should fully realize that our state is rapidly becoming an industrial area. At the same time, those not so interested in our natural resources should realize too, that sport and commercial expenditures and earnings in our state are as great, if not greater, than any single industry within our boundaries. Our primary aim should be to enhance and develop our natural resources to the fullest extent, compatable with the inevitable industrial growth of our state.

This is the challenge that faces you and me. A challenge that must be met by all outdoor interests, commercial, sportsmen and technical. Each division of the Wildlife and Fisheries Commission is charged with specific areas of responsibility. Each individual Commission employee is fully as important as the next in the discharge of those duties assigned to him. As a coordinated team, we will do all in our power to safeguard the natural resources of our state and make them more available to the people of the state.

In order to best serve all interests it is necessary that we have the full support and cooperation of all the citizens of the state.

My earnest appeal is for your help.

IN THIS ISSUE

Wetland Habitat Improvement 2

The Clapper Rail of Louisiana 5

Where are the Deer in Louisiana 8

Dove Kill Survey 11

Action Agents (photo feature)....................... 12

Hunting Outlook for Louisiana 14

Dr. Leslie Glasgow is named Director 15

Oil Field Waste in Saline Area 16

Freshwater Commercial Fishing 18

Commission Announces Hunting Seasons 21

Wildlife-O-Gram 24

Bird of Month ....Inside Back Cover

Wetlands Habitat Improvement

AMMONIUM NITRATE BLASTING AGENT

Ted Joanen

THE REDUCTION in wetland habitat throughout the United States and Canada as a result of drainage from increasing agricultural demands, oil development and housing projects has caused much concern among many public and private wildlife groups. Many kinds of wildlife depend upon or benefit from wetlands.

Much is being done on public lands to preserve our remaining wetlands, although this alone will not off-set declining habitat. The majority of our wetland areas are on private lands, and the cost of improving these areas for wildlife in many cases have been out of reach of the private landowner.

For the first time many landowners have the opportunity to improve relatively unproductive marshes at a cost within their means. The use of a relatively new and inexpensive blasting agent, ammonium nitrate and fuel oil, will permit landowners to enhance the value of their marshes as waterfowl habitat.

Ammonium nitrate is a common chemical fertilizer. It is not an explosive in itself but when mixed with a carbonaceous carrier such as fuel oil, and detonated with an explosive primer, it becomes an effective blasting agent having the same strength as dynamite. Although draglines and bulldozers are very effective in developing

Each 20 pound charge is carefully checked for possible leaks.

Forty-five 20-lb. bags of ammonium nitrate will be set in place to blast a pond 40 ft. x 50 ft. x 3 ft.

wildlife habitat, the cost of operating these machines and poor access often limit their use.

The mixture of ammonium nitrate and fuel oil is called a blasting agent rather than an explosive. A small amount of dynamite is used to provide the heat and shock needed to trigger the explosion which is actually a very rapid uniting of fuel with the oxygen in the ammonium nitrate.

Biologists of the Michigan and Wisconsin Conservation Departments and the United States Forest Service were among the first to use this blasting agent for wildlife habitat improvement. Results of their work on the Horicon Marsh in Wisconsin showed excellent use by mallards and blue-winged teal. Many deer, mink, pheasants and rabbits were found using potholes.

To better acquaint wildlife techniques in the Southeastern part of the United States with the use of this blasting agent, a demonstration was given recently on Horn Island National Wildlife Refuge and sponsored by the U. S. Fish & Wildlife Service, the Louisiana Wild Life and Fisheries Commission and the Louisiana State University School of Forestry and Wildlife Management. Ted

general upper limits that is advisable with many areas restricted to smaller charges because of nearby houses. One particularly bad practice occurring at times is the loading of excessive charges in the first shot to be tried without realizing what the consequences might be. Workers in Wisconsin have found that a 100

nitrate.

900 pounds of ammonium nitrate, equivalent to an equal weight of TNT, sends debris 200 feet in the air.

The explosive charge is placed just below the surface of the soil with the prima-cord detonator exposed. This is connected to other charges by means of another prima-cord trunkline.

pound charge may break windows over half a mile away. A strong wind blowing away from the axis of the charge will help keep debris from falling into the excavation and is especially helpful for large diameter holes. One disadvantage of using ammonium nitrate is that it must be kept dry. Charges are normally placed three to four feet below the surface of the ground and when used in marsh conditions, the ammonium nitrate must be sealed in waterproof bags. Water will render it ineffective as a blasting agent.

In general it is not possible to deepen fish

A small pot hole was blasted by using five 20-lb. charges.

ponds by blasting. Very large shots are seldom advisable. Ammonium nitrate blasting is best suited for making small potholes. One or two shots in a large temporarily dry pond may create deeper holes. Most of the blasted material, however, is deposited within a hundred feet and little actual deepening is accomplished. Longevity is likely to be very short if ponds are flooded since debris tends to settle in the deeper holes.

Blasting of a few potholes for habitat improvement does some good but if the program is to have a real impact on duck production potholes are needed in really large numbers. Breeding ducks like to move about for short distances during the breeding season even when not disturbed. Concentrations of potholes permit these movements and also encourage more ducks to use an area. Concentrations of potholes should also benefit broods by providing intermediate feeding and resting areas. A pothole spacing of 200-300 feet is recommended for intensive management. Also alligators, frogs, crawfish, and turtles can be easily encouraged if the potholes are in large enough numbers to supply the requirements of these forms of wildlife. Ammonium nitrate mix-

This is the pond which was created by detonating the 900 pounds of ammonium nitrate.

ture could probably be used to good advantage in the removal of complaint beaver dams by persons authorized to undertake this type of activity. By spacing the charges in a line, ditches can be produced by this method.

Ammonium nitrate—fuel oil mixtures are not classed as explosives, but as "blasting agents." They must be considered dangerous and handled or stored like any other high explosive. Their use should be supervised by someone experienced in the handling of explosives. ✹

(Editor Note)

Portions of this article have been taken from "Pothole Blasting for Wildlife", Wisconsin Conservation Department, 1965, by Harold A. Matkiak, and "Marsh Blasting with Ammonium Nitrate". Forest Service, U. S. Department of Agriculture and Michigan Department of Conservation by Robert Radthe, U. S. F. S. and John Byelich, M.D.C.

U. S. Fish and Wildlife Service Surveys Need for Hatchery Fish

A survey to determine future needs for hatchery fish to help manage the nation's fishing was announced recently by Secretary of the Interior Stewart L. Udall.

The survey will be made by the Department's Bureau of Sport Fisheries and Wildlife in cooperation with State fish and game departments. It will be used to estimate the water now suitable for sport fishes, how much of this is or should be stocked, fisherman numbers, future stocking needs, and capabilities of National, State, and private hatcheries. The survey is also expected to be helpful in deciding the future roles of public and private hatcheries.

In announcing the survey, Secretary Udall said data gathered will be projected to cover needs for "hatchery fish" in 1973, 1980, and 2000.

"The role of artificial production in providing for America's angling needs must be better defined," he said. "Stocking and production guidelines resulting from this survey are needed to keep up with the ever-increasing angling pressure while still maintaining or improving the quality of fishing."

Full cooperation from State game and fish departments was pledged in a letter to the Bureau of Sport Fisheries and Wildlife from William E. Towell of Missouri, president of the International Association of Game, Fish, and Conservation Commissioners.

Three More Camps Ready at Pass-a-Loutre Area

Plans are underway to provide Louisiana duck hunters the opportunity to utilize the Pass-a-Loutre Waterfowl Management Area again this season. Details of the over-all hunting program on Pass-a-Loutre will be published in the November-December issue of the CONSERVATIONIST.

Marsh conditions at the present time look very good in spite of the severe damages sustained by Hurricane Betsy last fall.

The three public camps destroyed by the hurricane are being rebuilt and will make a total of nine camps available to hunters utilizing the area this season. ✹

The muskrat, a common inhabitant of Louisiana's marshes, ranges in size from 16 to 25 inches. It lives in both salt and freshwater marshes. Its voice consists of squeals, squawks, snarls and groans. It is most active at night and it swims at 2-3 miles per hour. Its food consists of rootstocks and stems, cattails, roseau cane shoots, crabs and crayfish, ribbed mussels and some small fish.

THE CLAPPER RAIL OF LOUISIANA'S COASTAL MARSH

Hugh A. Bateman, Jr.

A Louisiana Clapper Rail with aluminum leg band attached. These game birds are one of several migratory species that remain underharvested in Louisiana due to lack of hunter interest and participation.

Game bird with a 70 day season and a daily bag limit of 15!!!

T0 THE LOCAL RESIDENTS of Louisiana's gulf coast the clapper rail *(Rallus longirostris)* is a "marsh hen" or "prairie hen". To the residents of Louisiana who live elsewhere and are unfamiliar with the bird life of our marshlands, the clapper rail is a "never heard of it" in a great majority of cases. For those who fall into the latter category, the clapper rail is a member of the Rallidae family which includes rails, gallinules and coots. The members of this family of birds are, in fact, responsible for the saying "thin as a rail". This quip is derived from the fact that rails are able to compress their bodies to the extreme laterally.

Nine species from the rail family are listed as occurring in Louisiana; six are true rails, two are gallinules, and one is a coot. Only two of these, the clapper and king rail *(Rallus elegans)*, are permanent residents of Louisiana. The other members are migratory and occur in number only as summer nesting or winter transits.

Of the six rail species the clapper and king rail are also the largest in Louisiana and are extremely similar in size and coloration. The clapper rail is restricted to saltwater environment while the king rail is a freshwater marsh and rice field dweller. Although there are differences, to be sure, for most purposes both of these rails are considered subject to the same considerations.

The remaining four species of rails are the Virginia rail *(Rallus limicola)*, sora rail *(Porzana carolina)*, yellow rail *(Coturnicops noveboracensis)*, and the black rail *(Laterallus jamaicensis)*. All of these small rails are extremely secretive, seldom seen and recognized only by experts in the field of bird study.

No doubt the best known representative of the rail family in Louisiana is the American coot *(Fulica americana)*, or better still the "poule d'eau". However, these slate-gray chicken-like fowl with white bills and a trusting nature ARE NOT subject to the same hunting regulations as are rails and gallinules. Coots are considered and classified as duck-type waterfowl and accordingly are subject to seasonal limitations set forth for ducks by the Federal Fish and Wildlife Service.

Gallinules are coot-like in shape but are much more brilliantly colored. The two species recorded from Louisiana's marshland are the common gallinule *(Gallinula chloropus)* and the purple gallinule *(Porphyralla martinica)*. These two birds are present in significant numbers only during the summer nesting season. The majority of gallinules leave Louisiana for tropical America in early fall before the gunning season opens.

Rails are rather unique in Louisiana for they fall within a group of migratory game birds, including woodcock and snipe, that are vastly underharvested in Louisiana. In recent years there has been an effort by professional wildlife people, both on a practicing and teaching level, to gain some insight into the ecology and present status of some of Louisiana's under-harvested species. In the face of recent restrictions of season length and allowable kill on some of our more popular waterfowl, such a program is surely appropriate.

From September, 1963 to June, 1965 the clapper rail was the subject of two years of basic research. The study was conducted on Grand Terre Island in Jefferson Parish, Louisiana. This island is surrounded by saltwater and is rather

Large scale trapping and banding programs are useful tools in detecting movement, hunting pressure, young/adult ratios, etc. Such information is valuable in properly managing any game species. The above trapped clapper rail was one of 108 such birds trapped, banded and released during a recent research study on rails in Louisiana.

typical of Louisiana's tremendous acreages of salt marsh, called home by the clapper rail.

The study was carried out through the correlated efforts of the Louisiana Wild Life and Fisheries Commission and the Louisiana Cooperative Wildlife Research Unit at L.S.U. Objectives accomplished involved an effective method for trapping rails, a suitable marking technique for identifying previously captured rails and an accurate method of sexing clapper rails

by body weight. In addition, food habits, nesting ecology, censusing techniques and internal parasitism were studied.

Specifically, the clapper rail is a rather drab, brownish-gray bird that approaches the size of a bantam chicken though not as plump. This rail is best characterized by a long, slightly decurved bill, short bobbed tail and long legs. By nature the clapper rail is quite secretive. Anyone who is the least familiar with our coastal marsh will agree that these birds are more often heard than seen. In fact, most people are astounded at the cackling clatter set forth across the marsh by first one and then many of these rails.

When undisturbed, the rail may be seen feeding along exposed mud flats and the banks of tidal ditches and canals. The rail relishes such areas for procuring its diet of small crabs, snails, insects, small fish and clams.

Nesting activities for the clapper rail usually begin in late March. In April six to twelve buffy eggs with reddish blotches are laid in a well concealed nest made of the surrounding grass. Both parents are thought to help incubate the eggs which hatch in 28-30 days. Only hours after hatching, young rails are very capable of fending for themselves. As soon as their downy plumage dries, they scamper off the nest to join their parents.

The solid black chicks remain with their parents for about six weeks and are flying in eight weeks. After 10 weeks young rails have become all but indistinguishable from adults in size and coloration.

A great many clapper rails are lost each year due to nest predation by Louisiana's tremendous

Louisiana's tremendous acreage of salt marsh that is available to clapper rails. This state's nearly three quarter million acres of salt marsh is unrivaled by that of any other state.

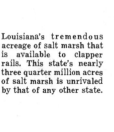

Although rails do their best work at running on the ground through thick marsh vegetation, one can see that they are quite at home in the water. Many times these birds choose to swim across small bodies of water rather than fly.

coastal population of raccoons, mink, skunks, etc. Additional losses to nests, young and adults are also expected where severe storms strike our Gulf Coast. However, the proven ability of clapper rails at renesting and raising multiple broods surely makes up for the natural losses that occur each year.

Most rail hunting is done in early morning and late evening hours and preferably during high tide since they are most active and apt to flush at these times. The most popular method of hunting rails in Louisiana employs the use of several people, several dogs, if available, and as much noise as possible. As many as four to six persons fan out abreast 30-40 yards apart. Several dogs of the retriever (not pointing) strain are then positioned to roam back and forth within gun range ahead of this line of hunters. The

The clapper rail is feeding in a tidal ditch at ebb tide. Such places are favorite to the rail in his efforts to catch stranded small fish, insects, clams, and small crabs.

whole group then begins a sweep across the marsh hollering and making as much noise as possible. This may sound a little ridiculous but rails are characteristicly weak fliers and are usually very reluctant to do so. All the encouragement possible is needed to make them rise clumsily to wing out the thick marsh grass. Once the victim is airborne, the shooting is easy as the rail offers no fancy aerial antics but lumbers off slowly in a straight line away from the hunters.

Since the shots had are usually at close range, an open bore 16 or 20 gauge gun is preferred using 7½ or 8 shot in light field loads.

The use of good dogs while hunting rails is essential if the hunter is to find a high percentage of downed birds. Rails are hardy and protectively

Clapper rail nests are usually well concealed in dense marsh vegetation near some source of water. This particular nest exhibits the typical canopy of grass over the top of the nest to help protect and conceal the eggs. The height of these nests above the floor of the marsh is normally sufficient to allow for the rising tides.

colored; and, though mortally wounded, a rail can move quickly quite a distance from a marked point and remain undetected.

As one might suspect, there are several obvious reasons for the rail's lack of popularity in Louisiana. Among the more important are: (1) rails are mostly confined to desolate and sparsely populated marshes; (2) few hunters are willing to make a long trip to these marshes during hot, mosquito type weather to hunt rails; (3) the soils of our marshes are usually soft and covered with thick, unyielding vegetation and are not suited to easy walking; (4) tide levels are insufficient to cover our marshes to a depth that will allow hunting by boat; (5) much of Louisiana's marshland is privately owned and not available for public hunting; and (6) these same

(Continued on page 10)

WHERE ARE THE DEER IN LOUISIANA?

John L. Haygood

ERE ARE THE RESULTS of our 1965-66 deer season by parishes. You can figure your parish's score compared to the rest of the state.

Deer kill information on the parish level has been long needed. Hunters have been asking for the kill by parish for years and the deer management section of the Louisiana Wild Life and Fisheries Commission says this information is a "must" for sound management and future planning. Trying to properly manage a deer herd without a parish by parish break down of the annual harvest is like trying to run a business without keeping books or records. Hunters can use this data to find out where the deer are and where hunting pressure is heaviest or lightest.

Louisiana's total reported deer kill for the 1965-66 season was 25,730. The big game license sales for the season were 82,505 and free old and underage permits were 28,587, which gave a grand total of 111,092 licenses issued. Only 97,758 of these license holders hunted and averaged 29.8 hunts for every deer killed.

Let's go back a ways and look at the history of Louisiana's deer hunting and deer management. During the early forties deer in huntable numbers could be found in only a few locations in the state. Practically all deer hunting was in the delta bottom lands of Madison, Tensas and Concordia Parishes, the upper Mississippi River, or in the deep swamps of the Atchafalaya and Maurepas regions. The deer restocking program was started in 1949 and in the following 15 years approximately 4,000 wild trapped deer were released.

Each release site was carefully selected by trained wildlife specialists, insuring the fact that the released deer had adequate range and good chance for survival and increase. Commission policy required that newly stocked areas remain closed to deer hunting for five years. This program paid off a thousand fold. In 1954 less than one half of Louisiana had deer hunting. By 1960 approximately two thirds of the state was open to hunting and now all parishes, except Acadia, have deer hunting. To better illustrate the increase, let's look at the 1960-61 seasons—the first year of the Big Game License. That year Louisiana sold 56,462 Big Game licenses and had a reported kill of 5,525 deer. Last year 82,505 licenses were sold and 25,730 deer were killed; an increase of 46 percent in hunters and 366 percent in deer kill.

But all is not peaches and cream; Louisiana is at a deer management crossroads. We have made the long pull getting the state adequately stocked; deer herds are well established. But field studies and the deer kill survey indicate a leveling off of deer herds in certain areas where we know the total potential is only one half achieved. Louisiana has 16,000,000 acres of commercial forest land and approximately 5,000,000 acres of marsh. The 16,000,000 acres of forest land will easily support one deer to every 60 acres for a deer herd potential of 266,000 deer. Good deer management indicates one third of a herd can be harvested annually. That means Louisiana could be harvesting at least 88,500 deer per year. All indications are that illegal hunting and free ranging dogs are holding herds in check. The only areas where deer herds reach the range potential are on wildlife management areas and posted

The Commission's numerous check stations located on wildlife management areas have been the only source for information leading to the number of deer killed in Louisiana. Current deer kill surveys provide a reliable parish by parish harvest which will be used to better manage the state's deer herds in future years.

lands. The difference between the management areas and posted hunting clubs on the one hand and the rest of the state on the other hand is better control of illegal hunting and of year around free ranging dogs in the former areas. To achieve Louisiana's deer hunting potential all sportsmen should support the efforts of our enforcement agents, abide by the hunting regulations and encourage their fellow hunters to do the same.

Table #1 lists the total results of the season. Note approximately 20 percent of the hunters bagged at least one deer, but only 1.5 percent killed three deer. The days hunted indicates the amount of recreation last years' deer season provided. This is important because providing hunting opportunity is one of the basic responsibilities of the Wild Life and Fisheries Commission.

Table I
Total Results of the 1965-66 Deer Season

Number of hunters	97,758
Days hunted	766,508
% of hunters killing *no* deer	80.5
% of hunters killing *one* deer	14.0
% of hunters killing *two* deer	4.0
% of hunters killing *three* deer	1.5
Total deer killed	25,730
Average days per hunter	7.8
Bucks killed	23,508
% Bucks	91
Does killed	2,222

Table #2 shows the information we are really looking for—harvest by parishes. The commercial forest acres column lists the basic deer range acreage of the parish, with the exception of coastal marsh parishes where non-forested wet lands provide the basic deer range. Look closely at the "deer kill within parish" column. You will notice that over a 1,000 deer were bagged in each of five parishes. Tensas was the high scorer with 3,759 deer bagged, Madison next with 3,210, Concordia third with 1,343 and Union fourth with 1,088. This Union Parish record is highly significant; it indicates what the people who are close to Louisiana's deer herds have been saying all along—deer hunting is moving to the hills. Twenty years ago, to go deer hunting one had to pack up his gear and head for the Delta. About ten years back deer seasons started opening up in the hill section. This was the result of restocking and excellent work by your enforcement men. Now, as you can see, hill parishes are beginning to contest the Delta's position as top deer country. To prove this let's look at our second ranking group of parishes that kill from 500 to 1,000 deer; they are Bienville 612, Bossier 570, Caldwell 879, Grant 731, Jackson 651, Morehouse 897, Natchitoches 757, Rapides 596 and Vernon 631. All of these are primarily upland deer country.

An interesting aspect of the survey shows where the hunters from any one parish killed their deer. There were 497 deer bagged in Ouachita Parish, but sportsmen from this parish led the state by harvesting a total of 2,339 deer by hunters away from home as well as locally. Many

THE RESULTS OF THE 1965-66 DEER SEASON BY PARISHES

Parish	Commercial Forest Acres	Deer Kill Within Parish	Forest Acres Per Deer Kill	No. of Hunters In Parish
Acadia	71,500	0		237
Allen	367,200	271	1,355	1,747
Ascension	103,700	57	1,819	605
Assumption	148,000	201	711	202
Avoyelles	313,500	308	1,018	1,282
Beauregard	661,200	117	5,651	1,282
Bienville	437,400	612	751	1,376
Bossier	414,000	570	726	2,118
Caddo	352,800	224	1,575	7,202
Calcasieu	244,200	60	4,070	3,005
Caldwell	305,000	879	347	1,666
Cameron**		29		104
Catahoula	345,000	211	1,635	1,534
Claiborne	365,800	313	1,168	1,246
Concordia	313,600	1,343	233	2,459
DeSoto	428,400	357	1,200	1,086
E. Baton Rouge	130,900	40	3,272	2,960
E. Carroll	109,200	1,051	104	1,271
E. Feliciana	161,000	14	11,500	202
Evangeline	219,600	179	1,227	1,054
Franklin	144,000	371	388	2,841
Grant	359,900	731	492	1,924
Iberia	115,000	147	782	330
Iberville	280,800	331	848	734
Jackson	335,000	651	514	1,903
Jefferson**		18		766
Jeff Davis	81,900	5	16,380	422
Lafayette	14,100	0		619
Lafourche	156,000	153	1,020	376
LaSalle	374,000	229	1,633	1,420
Lincoln	218,400	165	1,324	1,958
Livingston	358,400	162	2,212	1,571
Madison	244,800	3,210	76	1,494
Morehouse	291,500	897	325	3,786
Natchitoches	616,000	757	814	2,251
Orleans		0*		929
Ouachita	300,800	497	605	9,488
Plaquemines**		0*	0	0
Point Coupee	194,700	434	449	830
Rapides	621,600	596	1,043	5,907
Red River	174,000	128	1,359	746
Richland	149,100	322	463	2,569
Sabine	540,000	301	1,794	1,738
St. Bernard**		0*		94
St. Charles	68,800	123	559	258
St. Helena	203,000	96	2,114	310
St. James	85,500	98	872	198
St. John	93,800	166	565	160
St. Landry	255,000	135	1,889	1,504
St. Martin	310,000	76	4,079	158
St. Mary	143,000	214	668	629
St. Tammany	404,700	193	2,097	799
Tangipahoa	345,600	206	1,678	986
Tensas	230,100	3,759	61	1,266
Terrebonne	122,400	117	1,046	318
Union	489,700	1,088	450	2,559
Vermilion**		180		197
Vernon	736,700	631	1,167	3,193
Washington	280,800	127	2,211	1,127
Webster	295,800	353	838	2,387
W. Baton Rouge	69,300	55	1,260	318
W. Carroll	67,500	57	1,184	2,192
W. Feliciana	179,200	108	1,659	176
Winn	567,000	770	736	1,669
Unknown Parish of Kill		237		
TOTAL		25,730		97,758

*Season closed because of hurricane.
**Marsh land.

Franklin Parish hunters also hunted away from home: A total of 371 deer were bagged in Franklin but hunters from this parish took a total of 1,647 deer. Caddo hunters were third with a total of 1,304 deer harvested and 224 kills in Caddo. Rapides was fourth with 1,093 total; Madison was fifth with 1,080 kills by Madison license buyers, but Madison had a total of 3,210 deer

Deer hunting in Louisiana is an outdoor sport that has been handed down from generation to generation. Knowing where to go to find good deer range is an important factor in hunting success. This young deer hunter seems to have found the right range.

killed in that parish. So here is a case where people from other parishes killed more deer in the parish than local license buyers. Richland was sixth with 1,036 deer killed by Richland license buyers but only 322 deer killed in Richland Parish. All of this brings out the fact deer must be managed on a statewide basis, for hunters do not stick to their home parish. Deer hunting, deer management and deer control is a statewide affair and has to remain so if we are to continue progressing in this sport.

The column "Acres per deer killed" records the information that is particularly important to the deer managers, for this gets right down to the meat of deer production—how many forest acres does your parish require to provide one deer in the bag. The fewer acres required indicates better deer herds, unless they are allowed to increase to a point where they are detrimental to the deer range, the forest and agriculture.

The column entitled "No. of hunters in parish" is self explanatory. It indicates the number of deer hunters per parish, but does not necessarily mean that these hunters hunted in their home parish. It is interesting to note that Ouachita has more deer hunters than any other parish. This is due to the availability of good deer hunting in all directions from Monroe, the parish seat.

The influence of hurricane "Betsy" on the 1965-66 deer season is evidenced by the poor showing of the hard-hit parishes such as Jefferson, Plaquemines, St. Bernard, Orleans and probably others to a lesser degree. Field surveys indicate this was only a temporary set back and things should be back to near normal this season, barring another hurricane.

Louisiana is one of the leading deer states in this part of the South. This is due to the people's cooperation in deer conservation, hard and diligent work by our game agents and constant progress in our deer management programs.

The deer kill survey by parishes is our most important step toward future improvement and management of our deer herds.

Hunters of this state are to be commended on their cooperation in assisting the Commission in this survey.

CLAPPER RAIL
(Continued from page 7)

marshes offer unchallenged opportunity to hunt more popular species such as ducks and geese.

Past hunting seasons on rails have usually been set to open the first week in October and run for 50 days through the second or third week in November. Last year Louisiana was granted a longer season of 70 days, October 9 through December 15.

This fall the rail season has been set to open on the 5th of November and span the next 70 days, sunrise to sunset, through January 13, 1967. A late fall and winter season should offer several advantages over the early October and November season of past years. Obviously, the weather will be cooler and as well mosquitoes will be less active; marsh vegetation will not be as rank and rails will have less cover in which to hide; after the first several frosts have arrived and daily air temperatures drop, small crabs and insects will be much less abundant and rails will remain active for longer periods in search of food. Perhaps the most important advantage will be the fact that the rail season will now span both the goose and duck season. Now those ardent waterfowlers who visit the marsh solely in pursuit of ducks and/or geese can take a whack at hunting rail.

With a liberal daily bag of 15, quite a fine time can be had. So, try some rail hunting this coming season; you will be pleasantly surprised at the sport involved and as well at the manner in which the clapper rail will grace your cooking pot. ✦

Two young clapper rails that have just hatched from a clutch of five eggs. The white bill and black plumage are characteristic of all young rails. Within hours after hatching, young rails scamper into the marsh to be fed by the two parent birds.

1965-66 Hunting Season

DOVE KILL SURVEY

Larry Soileau

F OR THE THIRD consecutive year, the Louisiana Wild Life and Fisheries Commission has conducted a telephone survey in order to measure dove kill in the state. Persons selected at random from throughout the state were called by telephone at the end of each segment of the hunting season and questioned about their dove kill. The information obtained from these calls has enabled the Commission to estimate the harvest of doves in the state during the 1965-66 hunting season.

The estimated kill during this hunting season was the largest recorded during the past three years. An estimated total of 1,687,900 doves were killed by persons residing in households with a telephone. This figure far exceeds the harvest of approximately a million doves recorded during each of the previous two years. The kill was distributed among the season segments as follows:

1965-66 Season	Kill
September 4-14	407,800
October 9-November 7	731,500
December 18-January 15	548,600

The distribution of harvest among the season segments differed from the pattern set during the previous two years of the survey. During these years the largest kill occurred during the first segment of the season—a period when interest in dove hunting is probably highest and when doves are the only legal game in the state. During the past season, however, the pattern was reversed with the smallest kill occurring during the first

Data is carefully recorded as trapped birds are banded and released. Recovery information from banded doves has assisted in solving many of the problems regarding the migration and distribution of these birds.

or September segment. This kill of over 400,000 doves equaled that of past years, but the harvest during the October-November and December-January segments far exceeded that of the past.

This larger kill was probably the result of an increased number of doves in the state during the 1965-66 hunting season. This increase was reflected in the monthly inventory of doves in the state. This inventory, which is actually a record of the count of doves seen during daylight driving throughout the state, revealed a substantially larger than normal number of doves present in the state beginning in October and lasting through January. The reason for this increased fall population in the state is not readily evident. The inventory of breeding birds in the spring of 1965 revealed no increase in number. The increase in the Louisiana fall population of doves, therefore, was the result of better than

Dove hunting offers excellent outdoor sport for the entire family. The erratic darting of the mourning dove tests the skill of the most exacting marksman. These three teenagers appear to have caught on fast.

average reproduction with a resulting larger fall population or of optimum conditions in the state which attracted and held over through the winter an unusually large number of birds.

This larger harvest of doves in Louisiana has not adversely affected the breeding population in the Eastern Management Unit, an area composed of Louisiana and states east of the Mississippi River and the area which raises the doves which hunters bag. An inventory of the breeding population of the Eastern Management Unit this spring has revealed an increase in the number of birds present. If reproduction is normal and conditions in the state prove attractive to doves this fall and winter, Louisiana hunters should enjoy another excellent dove hunting season.

The Commission will again conduct a tele-

(Continued on page 20)

The initial planning and coordination of coastal patrol by enforcement personnel originate in the main office of the Louisiana Wild Life and Fisheries Commission in New Orleans.

Here illegally taken migratory waterfowl were seized and given to a children's orphanage.

Action

THE WILD LIFE and Fisheries Commission enforcement agent in pursuing his duties goes many places and meets many situations. He may be assigned to patrol in turbulent Gulf waters or may work in inland bayous and lakes or may enforce safety regulations and effect rescues; you name it and the law enforcement agent has done it or is prepared to do it.

Main aim of the Enforcement Division is to train each agent so that he is thoroughly familiar with his duties. Under a new program not only agents but most employees of the commission are able to attend a special school where they learn what the other fellow is doing and how he does it. This ranges from demonstrations and participation in karate and pistol use to the right way to make arrests and how to make the evidence "stick."

In pursuance of his duties the agent becomes familiar with every means of communication known to modern science from walkie-talkies, ship-to-shore radios and the like.

The game agent is the closest link to the general public in the area he serves. ✳

Confiscated game fish, taken by illegal means, were seized by alert Enforcement personnel and donated to charitable organizations.

The enforcement division maintains a constant vigil on Louisiana's Gulf waters to insure safe motorboat operations and to halt all violations that may occur.

Commission-owned airplanes are utilized on enforcement patrols and have proven to be a very valuable asset.

Agents!

When the fall hunting seasons roll around the enforcement agents are always there to check the bag limits and hunting licenses.

**Photo Feature
By
Robert N. Dennie**

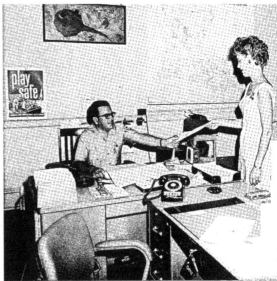

Complaints sent into the main office in New Orleans are quickly and efficiently processed and measures are taken to stop the violations.

The needed information is radioed to field personnel in mobile units so they may move in and take the necessary action.

The "Walkie Talkie" has proven to be a valuable tool in enforcement of game violation in the more remote areas of our state.

The patrol of inland waters is a never ending and necessary job to insure safe boat operation, and to prevent any violation of our state fishing laws.

Hunting Outlook

For Louisiana

T HE HUNTING outlooks for the 1966-67 dove, rabbit, deer, woodcock, rail and snipe seasons seem to be holding their own with those of the past season according to studies made in the field by the Louisiana Wild Life and Fisheries Commission.

Outlook for the squirrel season was somewhat problematical according to information from men in the various districts throughout the state.

It was indicated, however, that local hunting conditions are sometimes affected by unpredictable events which often tip the scales of hunter success one way or another. By this they referred to weather, habitat, hunting pressure and other future prevailing factors.

SQUIRRELS

Squirrel populations for the coming season should approximate those of last year. Although it is possible that due to poor mast conditions during the fall of 1965 squirrel reproduction during the following spring of 1966 may have been below normal. This, study leaders report, could naturally result in below average hunting populations in 1966.

They qualified that there is no need for squirrel hunters to be alarmed as conditions should improve in 1967 as an excellent mast crop is now in the offing.

It should be pointed out, that squirrel populations are cyclic, being directly proportional to food conditions of the previous fall. And that it only takes one or two years of abundant food to produce a bumper population of squirrels and that it should be emphasized that even though we are witnessing a "Low" in squirrel numbers "there is no need to alter our present bag limits and season. Research has shown that under current regulations gunning pressure has little influence on future population potentials."

DOVE

The annual survey of the breeding population of doves in Louisiana and the states east of the Mississippi River (the area which supports most of the doves which this state hunts) indicates an increase of four percent in the number of breeding birds in the spring of this year when compared to the spring of 1965. Since a high percentage of the fall kill is composed of the young of the year, the rate of production of young from this breeding population determines the number of doves available during the hunting season. No method has yet been developed to measure this production; therefore, forecast of the size of the fall population is now made on the strength of a measure of the breeding only.

A slightly smaller breeding population last spring ultimately resulted in the killing of more than a million and a half doves during the fall. During the past three years the dove kill in the state has ranged from approximately a million to over one and one-half million doves with a stable breeding population; therefore, if production equals that of the past several years, hunters can expect another excellent dove hunting season.

RABBITS

A very good rabbit hunting season is predicted because there is an abundance of rabbits in most of Louisiana where habitat is suitable. During the spring and summer months the rate of reproduction was high and this accounted for the many young rabbits that were visible in the late summer afternoons along country roads, railroads, highways, hedgerows and other similar places.

Of course, there will always be some hunters who go to their favorite spots. Some will find poor hunting success. There are always exceptions to the rule and consequently in a few areas the rabbit population will be low due to influences such as weather, inadequate food, poor cover, overabundance of predators, and parasites, or a combination of factors.

The overall outlook, however, is bright for rabbit hunters this fall.

DEER

Deer hunters can generally expect good prospects for the forthcoming 1966-67 deer season. However, there are several factors to consider in the overall success or failure of the deer hunter. Clearing of vast acreages of bottomland hardwoods, for agricultural purposes, over the past several years' has certainly had a drastic effect on the deer as well as the hunter. For the deer this reduction of habitat left it without its natural preferred deer browse plants and mast and now the hunter in some cases will have to find another place to do his hunting.

Weather demands great consideration in the hunting of deer. Excessive rainfall will affect the number of deer taken especially in low areas where hunting with dogs is permitted. High water may also limit access to the deer. Low temperatures will keep some prospective deer hunters close to the fire rather than in the woods and thereby result in a lower harvest. Hot and dry weather will cut down on the effectiveness of dogs where they are used.

Game Management areas scattered throughout the state will provide excellent opportunities for the deer hunting public. Hunting regulations on these areas should once again allow an optimum harvest of the deer herds. The overall number of deer killed on the Game Management Areas will not be as high this year as in the past. This will be due to the loss of the Chicago Mills Game Management Area where 1,400 or more deer of either sex season have been killed.

Archery hunting which has gained in popular-

(Continued on page 15)

DR. LESLIE GLASGOW IS NAMED DIRECTOR

D R. LESLIE L. GLASGOW, professor of wildlife
management at Louisiana State University,
was named director of the Wild Life and
Fisheries Commission at a meeting held in Baton
Rouge on August 2. He replaces J. D. Hair, Jr.
of Baton Rouge who resigned. Glasgow's appoint-
ment became effective as of August 16.

A native of Portland, Indiana, Dr. Glasgow
has been connected with the LSU school of forestry and wildlife management since 1948. He
was named a full professor in 1964. He has received national acclaim for his research and pub-
lications on the woodcock in Louisiana.

The new director received a bachelor of science
degree in forestry and wildlife management from
Purdue University in 1942; a master of science
degree in wildlife conservation from the University of Maine in 1948. His doctorate in game
management was awarded by Texas A&M University in 1958.

Because of his dedicated interest in the wise use
and management of the state's wildlife resources,
the Louisiana Outdoor Writers Association pre-
sented Dr. Glasgow with its outstanding conservationist award in 1958. As a member of the National Wildlife Society he has served in various
capacities including chairman of the Southeastern
region.

Dr. Glasgow has also conducted research on
nutria, effect of pesticides on wildlife populations
and ecological studies of the Louisiana marshes.
He is the author of numerous professional writ-
ings including an article on the Barn Owl which
appeared in the December 1959 issue of the LOU-

ISIANA CONSERVATIONIST. He is co-author
with Lavon A. McCollugh of a pamphlet, entitled
"Nutria for Home Use" published by the LSU
Agricultural Experiment Station in cooperation
with the Wild Life and Fisheries Commission.

Director Glasgow is married to the former
Garnet Confer; is the father of three sons and
resides at 663 Sunset Boulevard in Baton
Rouge. ✠

HUNTING OUTLOOK
(Continued from page 14)

ity in recent years, should see an increase in participation. This, plus liberal regulations, should
provide the highest bow hunter kill yet.

Generally the deer hunter should fare well
during the approaching season.

QUAIL

Louisiana quail hunters can expect about the
same size quail population as was present at the
opening of the 1965-66 season.

Some local areas in the northern and western
parts of the state have been deficient in rainfall throughout June and July. Here quail production will be below normal. Some other areas have
had a good pattern of summer rainfall affording
excellent brood production.

Quail habitat has continued to deteriorate in
many areas of the state due to intensified demands for other uses for the land.

RAILS AND SNIPE

Marsh conditions during the spring and summer have been favorable for the production of
rails in the Louisiana marshes. Increased production along with a change in hunting regulations
should allow the sportsmen who hunt in the
marsh country to enjoy a larger bag. The later

season will also allow hunting over marsh which
has been burned—a condition which was not possible during the former seasons.

No information is available on snipe production for the coming season. These birds are migratory and hunter success will depend largely
on the amount of rainfall which might occur
just prior to the hunting season. The snipe re-
quires moist soil conditions to allow him to probe
for his food.

WOODCOCK

Some quail hunters, some rabbit hunters, and
indeed a few out-and-out woodcock hunters look
forward to the annual opening of woodcock seasons in Louisiana. The popularity of this big-
eyed long-beaked bird that uses moist thickets by
day and open grassy areas at night has recently
increased in the eyes of some Louisiana hunters.

The daily bag increase of from four to five a
few years back, and season framework exten-
sion through January 30 by the Bureau of Sport
Fisheries and Wildlife, has allowed the Commission to set regulations that allow interested hunters to better utilize the woodcock resource. De-
spite evidence of increased kills by hunters up
and down the U.S. and Canada the continental
woodcock populations remain at a healthy high
level. ✠

The above picture shows an old salt burn which occurred on the Saline Wildlife Management Area before it was acquired by the Commission. These burns are caused by salt water which has been allowed in the past to flow uncontrolled. Only time and careful management will restore this area to its former beauty and wildlife productiveness.

Oil Field Waste Pollution Abatement
In The
Saline Wildlife Management Area

Robert Lafleur

IN FEBRUARY 1965, as a part of our statewide program of pollution abatement, personnel of the Division of Water Pollution Control of the Louisiana Wild Life and Fisheries Commission conducted a lease-by-lease inspection of oil fields, LaSalle and Catahoula parishes, located in or adjacent to the Saline Wildlife Management Area.

Oil fields located within the area are: Sandy Bayou, West Saline Lake, Cypress, North Big Island, Catahoula, South Catahoula, Long Slough, North Saline, Indian Bayou, Big Bayou Field was included in the inspection because it is adjacent to the management area and any wastes lost from this field would, in all probability, result in pollutional damage.

A detailed report was prepared following the inspection. Correspondence, accompanied by a copy of the report, was directed to all operators of oil producing installations requesting that, where necessary, remedial measures be initiated at the earliest possible date. This correspondence also requested information relative to what remedial measures would be taken as well as an expected date of completion of these corrective actions.

Responses to this office were quite gratifying. The majority of the oil operators had already taken steps, or were in the process of completing necessary measures—within the limits of practicability—to prevent pollution of streams and land areas from salt water and waste oil.

In April and May of 1966 representatives of the Louisiana Wild Life and Fisheries Commission and of the Louisiana Department of Conservation met with oil operators involved to discuss oil spillage and salt water problems on the Commission owned Saline Wildlife Management Area. The plans of the Louisiana Wild Life and Fisheries Commission to enhance, improve, and develop this 60,000 acre tract in every way possible to make it an attractive public hunting, fishing, and outdoor recreational area were indicated at meetings and later emphasized by letter to each operator. In this endeavor the Commission has requested that all oil operators within or adjacent to the area cooperate as follows: (1) Replace all deteriorated oil lines to prevent or reduce the large number of line breaks that can be anticipated. (2) Frequent inspections of all trunk and feeder lines to prevent oil spillage. (3) Immediately notify, if possible, certain personnel of the Louisiana Wild Life and Fisheries Commission and the Louisiana Department of Conservation in the event of accidental oil spills or salt water discharges. (The Louisiana Wild Life and Fisheries Commission is interested in preventing water pollution as well as preventing the destruction of timber by burning.) (4) Prevent any salt water, drilling mud, oil base or otherwise, from being discharged to any land area or into any stream, bayou, lake, or other waters in the Saline Wild Life Management Area or adjacent areas. (5) Where leaks occur, restore area to original appearance prior to spillage. (6) Maintain slush pits on the area in good condition to prevent overflow or leakage of any waste oil, salt water, or other noxious or contaminating materials. (7) Restore dry hole sites to original condition.

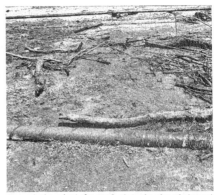

One of the giant forward steps in the abatement of water pollution is being accomplished by the Louisiana Wild Life and Fisheries Commission's Division of Water Pollution Control on its Saline Wildlife Management Area in LaSalle and Catahoula parishes. A majority of oil operators have taken steps to prevent pollution of streams and land areas from salt water and waste oil. In the above picture old oil lines have been replaced and inspection may be accomplished readily as spills occur.

All employees of the Louisiana Wild Life and Fisheries Commission who work in or around the Saline Wildlife Management Area have been instructed to assist in every way possible to enable oil operators to accomplish the aforementioned recommendations.

The pollution enforcement arms of the Louisiana Wild Life and Fisheries Commission and the Louisiana Department of Conservation will maintain surveillance in the area and rigorously enforce anti-pollution laws, rules, and regulations. ✺

Pipe breaks, such as the one above, are a hazard to fish and wildlife, and companies operating in the Saline Wildlife Management Area have agreed to pick up all of the oil possible when such breaks occur and restore the terrain to its original appearance.

A Declining Industry!
FRESHWATER COMMERCIAL FISHING

Lloyd Posey

LIKE THE OLD GRAY MARE, "it ain't what it used to be". The freshwater commercial fishing industry of Louisiana is slowly dying. Let's briefly examine the state of the industry, try to determine the causes of the decline, and possibly make some predictions about the future.

At one time Louisiana had an ideal environment for the production of commercial fish. The annual flooding or backwater covering rich bottom land provided ideal spawning and feeding areas. Commercial fish were abundant and were harvested in amazing quantities. Fishing was an important part of our economy.

Over the years changes have occurred in the ecology of our state. First came levees to retard flood waters. Then canals and drainage ditches were created to drain marginal lands. Gradually these changes and others have severely limited the natural flooding and dewatering cycle in many areas. Commercial fish were denied spawning and nursery areas. Food supplies dwindled. Channelized streams dried up in the summer. Upstream dams retarded flows. The ideal environment for fish, frogs, and crayfish was destroyed.

Freshwater fishing is the backbone of many small communities in Louisiana. Pollution has taken its toll of our freshwater fishing industry and experts say that fishermen, such as this one seen with his hoop net, will no longer be seen in our inland waters unless something is done fast.

Due to pollution and man-made changes in streams and lakes, catches of fresh water fish such as the buffalo fish, seen above, are becoming more difficult to obtain. Biologists say the freshwater commercial fisheries of Louisiana are slowly dying.

Pollution has had a tremendous impact upon our fishery resources. Salt water, waste oil and other harmful substances flowed into our streams, killing fish and food organisms. Many streams and lakes in northwest and central Louisiana were affected.

Effluent from industry and sewerage from large cities found its way, untreated, into our rivers and streams. Both took a heavy toll. In recent years great advances have been made in pollution control, but recovery will be a slow process.

The development of powerful new insecticides since World War II has seriously affected our fish and wildlife resources. Some of these materials have entered our streams, killing vast quantities of fish. For example, in the early 1960's the commercial fish in the Mississippi River were severely decimated by endrin. This is a powerful chlorinated hydrocarbon commonly used in control of insects damaging cotton and sugar cane. It can kill fish at concentrations of less than one part of chemical in a billion parts of water. This was a severe blow since the Mississippi River is the primary source of supply for many important fishing areas. Dead fish were found from the Arkansas line to the Gulf.

At one time the primary areas of concentration for commercial fishing were our large rivers and associated tributaries and backwater areas. These have been seriously affected by the previously mentioned causes and by subsequent decline in available commercial fish. Lake fisheries have not been so seriously affected. In fact, production is very good in some lakes such as Lake Verret and Lac des Allemands.

Another cause of decline, not so well known, is the fishermen themselves. They resist change. Most are reluctant to modernize and streamline their operations. They fail to take advantage of new gear developments. In many cases they are still using techniques which were common two thousand years ago.

Fishermen have not searched for unexploited fishery resources. In the Great Lakes, trash fish such as chubs are utilized. These are taken with modern stern ramp trawlers and sold to canneries for making pet foods. We have species in Louisiana that could stand considerable exploitation: the gizzard shad, for instance. These shad constitute from 50 to 85 percent of the entire fish population, by weight, in some lakes.

They have been reluctant to seek new and better markets for the fish they catch. More consistent and higher prices could be obtained by establishing midwest and western outlets for their products. Fish are in demand there and bring much better prices than in the south.

Commercial fishermen in some areas of our state have opposed sound biological management principles. They fail to realize that commercial fish are a renewable resource and that the surplus can be harvested. They have succeeded in closing large areas to any gear other than trotlines. This leaves a large segment of the fishery unexploited. This is detrimental to the economy as well as the ecology of an area. Exploitation of a single or perhaps two species is unrealistic and unsound.

The Louisiana Wild Life and Fisheries Commission conducted an extensive study of commercial fishing gear and its effect on fish populations. Recommendations were made to the legislature and most were adopted. The recommendations were designed to allow maximum utilization of the resource without endangering brook stock.

All of these recommendations, however, have not been accepted. The slat trap, an efficient device which captures catfish, is illegal. Extensive studies have shown that the catch in this gear is better than 98% catfish. They can be used with no danger to game fish populations.

Uninformed sport fishermen have caused areas to be completely closed to commercial fishing. By doing so, they are lessening their chances of making a good catch. When commercial fish are under-harvested, game fish populations decline due to competition for food and space. Stable lakes with high commercial and rough fish populations do not produce good sport fishing. Some progress has been made toward making sport fishermen aware of the need for commercial fishing, but much remains to be done.

All of these factors have combined to slowly strangle the freshwater commercial fishing in-

These channel catfish were taken by commercial fishermen and are prized nationwide; however, effluent from industry and sewage from large cities and waste matter of all kinds has found its way into our fresh waters and is doing away with catches such as this one.

This is a fine catch of prized flathead catfish taken from Lac des Allemands and may be among the last if pollution is allowed to continue in our freshwaters. In fact, fishing is still good in the lakes, but if allowed to spread, pollution will eventually do away with the good fishing here, there and elsewhere.

dustry. There are fewer persons, in relation to total population, engaged in fishing and related occupations than there were ten years ago. Many fishermen have quit fishing and taken industrial jobs. The older ones continue to fish, but their numbers are decreasing each year and there is little recruitment. The young men can make a better living elsewhere and show little interest in commercial fishing. The industry is not dead yet by any means, but the decline is steady. It is just a matter of time.

What can we expect in the future? It seems likely that the decline will continue until the commercial fishing industry is a mere remnant of its former size. However, a new and exciting industry is arising to take its place. Commercial production of pond-reared fish, or fish farming, is expanding rapidly. It has many advantages over commercial fishing. Fish farmers can closely control the environment to produce the species, size and quantity of fish needed. These farm-reared fish are of excellent quality. They may be harvested at the time when the market is most favorable.

Production is amazing. For example, between 1,500 and 2,000 pounds of catfish can be produced in a one-acre pond each year with proper management. Experiments are being conducted with hybrids with the hope of producing faster growing fish which require less food. As experience is gained in this field, production will increase and costs will go down. A word of caution at this point—new fish farmers should proceed on a limited scale until they learn their production techniques. It is suggested that a new operation should not exceed 8-10 acres.

The market for farm-reared fish is unlimited.

Many are sold alive for stocking, pay fishing lakes. Others are shipped to markets all over the country. The demand far exceeds the present supply. Declining landings of fresh and saltwater commercial fish will increase the demand for farm reared fish even more in coming years.

It is regrettable that our commercial fishermen are a disappearing breed. When they are gone, a colorful chapter in the history of Louisiana will close. They will be replaced by modern fish farmers cognizant of the economics and biology of fish production.   ✻

DOVE KILL SURVEY
(Continued from page 11)

phone survey following the 1966-67 hunting season in order to estimate kill. This year, however, the survey will be conducted in all southeastern states with calls originating from Raleigh, North Carolina. The acceptance and adoption by other states of the telephone survey as a method of estimating dove kill is the result of many years of basic research by the Game Research Project of the Louisiana Wild Life and Fisheries Commission. Pioneering efforts begun in Acadia Parish in 1960 resulted in the first statewide dove kill estimation by the use of a telephone based survey in 1963-64. The results of this survey were reported in the May-June, 1964 "Louisiana Conservationist."

Thus, the development of the telephone kill survey has added another tool to the growing bag of techniques now being used by dove researchers to better manage the mourning dove resource.   ✻

Where to go for the gray ghosts is a conversation piece throughout Louisiana beginning in early September. This seems to have been a good spot. A corn field harvested by mechanical pickers leaves ample food for doves and if there is a water hole nearby, then the shooting should be even better.

COMMISSION ANNOUNCES HUNTING SEASONS

1966-67 HUNTING SEASONS

Seasons and bag limits on doves, snipe, woodcock, rails and gallinules and established the seasons and bag limits for quail, rabbits, squirrel, deer, bear and turkey.

RESIDENT GAME BIRDS AND ANIMALS

(Shooting Hours—one-half hour before sunrise to one-half hour after sunset)

Quail: November 24—February 28; Daily Bag 10; Possession 20.

Rabbit: October 1—February 28; Daily Bag 8; Possession 16.

Squirrel: October 1—January 10; Daily Bag 8; Possession 16.

Bear: Closed

Turkey: April 1—April 23; Daily Bag 1, Gobblers only; Season Limit 1. See schedule.

Deer: See Deer Hunting Schedule.

Archery Season: October 8—November 20, 1966, Inclusive (See Deer Hunting Schedule)

Commercial Hunting Preserves; October 1—March 31, Pen-raised birds only.

1966-67 MIGRATORY REGULATIONS

Doves: 3 way split: September 3-September 18, 16 days; October 15-November 6, 23 days; December 16-January 15, 31 days; Bag Limit 12; Possession 24.

Teal: Experimental Season, September 17-September 25, Daily Bag limit 4, possession 8, Blue-Winged and Green-Winged Teal only. Each hunter must have in possession while hunting:

1. Special teal hunting permit (application deadline August 17).
2. Basic hunting license or State hunting permit except persons under 16 years of age.
3. Federal duck stamp except persons under 16 years of age.

Rails and Gallinules: November 5-January 13, 1967; Bag limit 15; Possession 30. Singly or in the aggregate of all species.

Woodcock: December 10-January 28, 1967, Bag limit 5; Possession 10.

Snipe (Wilson's): November 26-January 14; Bag limit 8; Possession 16.

SHOOTING HOURS:

1. Doves: 12:00 noon to sunset.
2. Rails, Gallinules, Snipe and Woodcock; sunrise to sunset.

1967 TURKEY SCHEDULE

Turkey: April 1-23 inclusive. Bag 1 gobbler per season. May be taken by still hunting only; the use of dogs and baiting being specifically prohibited. Open only in the following areas:

AREA NO. A—Union and Morehouse Parishes. East of La. Hwy. 549 from Arkansas line to La. Hwy. 348 at Conway; North of La. Hwys. 348 and 33 from Conway to Marion; east of La. Hwys. 143 and 2 from Marion to Ouachita River; west of Ouachita River from La. Hwy. 2 to the intersection of Parish Road and Ouachita River (south of Papaw Lake); north of Parish Road and La. Hwy. 592 from Ouachita River to U. S. Hwy. 165; north of U. S. Hwy. 165 from La. Hwy. 592 to La. Hwy. 139; west of La. Hwys. 139 and 140 from Bastrop to Bonita; west of U. S. Hwy. 165 from Bonita to Arkansas line; except the Union Parish Game Management Area. See Game Management Area Schedule for Georgia-Pacific Wildlife Management Area.

AREA NO. B—Madison, Franklin, Catahoula, Concordia and Tensas Parishes. South of U. S. Hwy. 80 from the Mississippi River to La. Hwy. 17. East of La. Hwys. 17 and 15 from Delhi to Winnsboro to Clayton; east and north of U. S. Hwy. 65 from Clayton to the Mississippi River.

AREA NO. C—East Feliciana, East Baton Rouge, Livingston, St. Helena and Tangipahoa Parishes. East of Thompson Creek from the Mississippi line to La. Hwy. 10; north of La. Hwy. 10 from Thompson Creek to Clinton; east of La. Hwy. 67 from Clinton to the junction of U. S. Hwy. 190 at Baton Rouge; north of U. S. Hwy. 190 from La. Hwy. 67 to the Amite River; east of Amite River from U. S. Hwy. 190 to Lake Maurepas; north of Lake Maurepas from Amite River to U. S. Hwy. 51; and west of U. S. Hwy. 51 from Lake Maurepas to the Mississippi State Line.

AREA NO. D—Washington and St. Tammany Parishes. East of La. Hwy. 25 from the Mississippi State Line to Covington; east and north of U. S. Hwy. 190 from Covington to the junction of U. S. Hwy. 90; and north of U. S. Hwy. 90 from the junction with U. S. Hwy. 190 to the Mississippi State Line.

1966-67 DEER HUNTING SCHEDULE

A. **Bag:** One legal deer per day; 3 legal deer per season.

B. Legal deer is defined as a deer with antlers not less than three inches in length. The killing of bucks with antlers less than three inches and doe deer is prohibited except where specifically permitted.

C. Deer hunting restricted to legal bucks only, except where otherwise specifically permitted.

D. Either sex deer, or any deer, is defined as any male or female deer, except spotted fawns which are protected, taken in any area designated and regulated as such.

E. Still Hunting Only prohibits the use of dogs for hunting or the training of dogs in areas so designated, including game management or refuge areas. In all other areas, deer hunting will be permitted with or without the use of dogs.

F. All areas not specifically designated as being open are hereby closed.

G. Archery season: October 8-November 20, 1966.

The taking of deer permitted in all areas declared open for deer hunting, including all game management areas except the following: Zemurray*, Thistlewaite and Concordia. Either sex deer may be taken in all open areas except in Catahoula, East Carroll, East Feliciana, Evangeline, Grant, Jackson, La-Salle, Livingston, Pointe Coupee, Sabine, St. Tammany, Rapides, Vernon, Washington, Webster, and Winn Parishes. Season permits required for hunting on game management areas. For details, see provisions under game management schedule. Special bow and arrow regulations: Arrows used for hunting deer shall have well sharpened metal broadhead blades not less than 7/8 inch in width.

The following shall be unlawful:

1. To have in possession any gun while hunting with bow and arrow during the special bow and arrow deer season.

2. To have in possession, or under control while hunting, any poisoned arrows, arrows with explosive tips, or any bow drawn, held or released by mechanical means.

3. To hunt deer with a bow having a pull less than 30 pounds.

*See Game Management Area Schedule

DESCRIPTION OF AREAS

40 days with or without dogs: November 25—December 18; December 26—January 10, 1967

AREA NO. 1: All or parts of Madison*, Franklin, Tensas*, Catahoula**, Concordia, Avoyelles, St. Landry, Pointe Coupee, West Feliciana, East Baton Rouge (Profit Island), West Baton Rouge, Lafayette, St. Martin, Iberville, Vermilion, Iberia, Assumption, St. Mary, Ascension, St. James, St. John, Terrebonne, Lafourche, St. Charles, Jefferson, Plaquemines, St. Bernard, Orleans, St. Tammany, Tangipahoa and Livingston. South of La. Hwy. 14 from Cameron-Vermilion Parish line to New Iberia, east of U. S. Hwy. 90 from New Iberia to Lafayette, east of U. S. Hwy. 167 from Lafayette to Opelousas, south of U. S. Hwy. 190 from Opelousas to junction of U. S. Hwy. 71, east of U. S. Hwy. 71 from U. S. Hwy. 190 to Bunkie, south and east of La. Hwy. 115 from Bunkie to Marksville to Effie to Big Creek, south of Big Creek and Old Saline Bayou to the Red River, south and west of Red River from La. Hwy. 115 to junction of Black River, east of the Black and Ouachita Rivers from Jonesville to Bouet River to Deer Creek, east of Deer Creek to La. Hwy. 15, east of La. Hwy. 15 from Winnsboro, east of La. Hwy. 17 from Winnsboro to U. S. Hwy. 80 at Delhi, south of U. S. Hwy. 80 from Delhi to the Mississippi River, West of Mississippi River from U. S. Hwy. 80 to La. Hwy. 22 (Ascension Parish) south of La. Hwy. 22 from Mississippi River to Sorrento to Springfield to the Tchefuncte River, west of the Tchefuncte River from La. Hwy. 22 to Lake Pontchartrain, west and south of Lake Pontchartrain to Lake Borgne, south and east of Lake Borgne to the Mississippi Sound. Included is Profit Island in East Baton Rouge Parish. EXCEPT that area designated as No. 15 which is Still Hunting Only.

33 days with or without dogs: November 25—December 11; December 26—January 10, 1967.

AREA NO. 2: All or parts of Madison, East Carroll, West Carroll, Morehouse, Richland and Ouachita. North of U. S. Hwy. 80 from Mississippi State Line to Hwy. 17 at Delhi, east of La. Hwy. 17 to Pioneer, north of La. Hwy. 588 from Pioneer to Boeuf River, west of Boeuf River to La. Hwy. 134, north of La. Hwy. 134 to La. Hwy. 133 at Oak Ridge, west of La. Hwy. 133 from Oak Ridge to U. S. Hwy. 80, north of U. S. Hwy. 80 from La. Hwy. 133 to Bayou Lafourche, east of Bayou Lafourche to Little Bayou Boeuf, east and north of Little Bayou Boeuf to La. Hwy. 2 at Perryville, north and west of La. Hwy. 2 from Perryville to the Ouachita River at Sterlington, east of

*The taking of either sex deer will be legal during the first five days of the regular season in that portion of Madison Parish south of U. S. Hwy. 80 extending to the Madison-Tensas Parish line, bounded on the west by State Route 577 to Bayou Macon, on the east by U. S. Hwy. 65 from Tallulah south to Turntable Road (Hwy. 603) by Turntable Road to the Sevier-Watts Road (Madison Parish Road 611), and along the Sevier-Watts Road to Madison-Tensas line. In addition, that area known as Sargent's Point in Madison Parish will be open to either sex deer hunting. All of Tensas Parish except Wards 3 and 5 will be open to the taking of either sex deer during the first five days.

**All lands lying within the boundary of the Saline Wildlife Management Area are subject to the same regulations as established for the Saline Wildlife Management Area proper.

Ouachita River to Arkansas Line.
AREA NO. 3: All or parts of Jackson. Winn, Grant, Rapides, Caldwell, Concordia, Bienville and LaSalle Parishes.
North of Big Creek from La. Hwy. 115 to Junction of Rapides-Avoyelles Parish Line, west of Rapides-Avoyelles Parish Line to Red River, north and east of Red River to mouth of Saline Bayou, east of Saline Bayou to Black Lake Bayou, east of Black Lake Bayou to La. Hwy. 155, south of La. Hwy. 155 to Saline, west of La. Hwy. 9 to Junction of La. Hwy. 126, south of La. Hwy. 126 to Dugdemona Bayou, east of Dugdemona Bayou to La. Hwy. 4, south of La. Hwy. 4 from Dugdemona Bayou to Jonesboro to Chatham to Vixen, west of Parish Road from Vixen to La. Hwy. 126, north of La. Hwy. 126 to La. Hwy. 127, west of La. Hwy. 127 to U. S. Hwy. 165, west of U. S. Hwy. 165 to Little River, west of Little River and Saline Bayou to La. Hwy. 28, south of La. Hwy. 28 from Saline Bayou to junction of U. S. Hwy. 84, south and east of U. S. Hwy. 84 to Black River, west of Black River to Red River. north of Red River from Black River to Old Saline Bayou, east and north of Old Saline Bayou to Big Creek to La. Hwy. 115.
AREA NO. 4: All or parts of Rapides, Beauregard, Allen, Evangeline, St. Landry, Vernon and Avoyelles Parishes.
South and east of La. Hwys. 28, 112, 113 and 112 from Alexandria to Union Hill through Pitkin to Sugartown to U.S. Hwy. 171; east of U. S. Hwy. 171 from La. Hwy. 112 to Ragley, north of U. S. Hwy. 190 from Ragley to Opelousas; east of U. S. Hwy. 167 from Opelousas to Ville Platte, west of La. Hwy. 29 from Ville Platte to Bunkie, west of U. S. Hwy. 71 from Bunkie to Alexandria.
AREA NO. 5: All or parts of Beauregard and Calcasieu Parishes.
South of Anacoco Bayou from the Texas line to La. Hwy. 111, west of La. Hwy. 111 to U. S. Hwy. 190, South of U. S. Hwy. 190 from La. Hwy. 111 to DeRidder; west of La. Hwy. 27 from DeRidder to Sulphur and north of U. S. Hwy. 90 from Sulphur to the Texas line.
AREA NO. 6: All or parts of Sabine, DeSoto and Vernon Parishes.
South of U. S. Hwy. 84 from Texas line to Logansport to Mansfield, west of U. S. Hwy. 171 from Mansfield to Leesville, north of La. Hwy. 8 from Leesville to Burr Ferry to Texas line.
AREA NO. 7: All or parts of Natchitoches and Red River Parishes.
South of La. Hwy. 174 from Ajax to intersection of La. Hwy. 1, east of La. Hwy. 1 to intersection of U. S. Hwy. 84 at Armstead, south and west of U. S. Hwy. 84 and U. S. Hwy. 71 from Armstead to Clarence, north and west of La. Hwy. 6 from Clarence to Natchitoches, west of La. Hwy. 1 from Natchitoches to Derry, west of La. Hwy. 119 from Derry to Gorum; north and west of the Kisatchie-Mink-Gorum Road (La. Hwy. 118) to Kisatchie, east of La. Hwy. 117 from Kisatchie to Vowell's Mill Road; north and east of Vowell's Mill Road (La. Hwy. 478) to Robeline, north and east of La. Hwy. 120 from Robeline to La. Hwy. 1221, east of La. Hwy. 1221 to La. Hwy. 174, south of La. Hwy. 174 to Ajax.
24 days with or without dogs:
November 25—December 4;
December 26—January 8, 1967.

AREA NO. 8: All or parts of Winn, Jackson, Caldwell, Ouachita, Franklin, Catahoula, LaSalle, Union, Lincoln, and Richland Parishes.
West of Ouachita River from Arkansas line to Sterlington, south of La. Hwy. 2 from Sterlington to Perryville, south and west of Little Boeuf Bayou from Perryville to Lafourche Drainage Canal, west of Lafourche Drainage Canal to U. S. Hwy. 80, south of U. S. Hwy. 80 to La. Hwy. 133, east of La. Hwy. 133 to La. Hwy. 134, south of La. Hwy. 134 to La. Hwy. 183, west of La. Hwy. 183 to U.S. Hwy. 80, north of U. S. Hwy. 80 from Holly Ridge to Rayville, west of La. Hwy. 137 from Rayville to Archibald, west of La. Hwy. 15 from Archibald to Deer Creek, west of Deer Creek and Ouachita river to Jonesville, north of U. S. Hwy. 84 from Jonesville to La. Hwy. 28, north of La. Hwy. 28, to Saline Bayou, east of Saline Bayou and Little River to junction of U. S. Hwy. 165, east of U. S. Hwy. 165 from Little River to junction of La. Hwy. 127, north of La. 127 to junction of La. Hwy. 126, south of La. Hwy. 126 to Parish Road from Chester to Vixen, north of La. Hwy. 4 from Vixen to Jonesboro, east of U. S. Hwy. 167 from Jonesboro to Arkansas line.
AREA NO. 9: All or parts of Sabine, Vernon and Natchitoches Parishes.
East of U. S. Hwy. 171 from Converse to Leesville, west of La. Hwy. 117 from Leesville to La. Hwy. 478, south and west of La. Hwy. 478 from La. Hwy. 117 to Robeline, west and south of La. Hwy. 120 from Robeline to La. Hwy. 1221, west of La. Hwy. 1221 to La. Hwy. 174, south of La. Hwy. 174 to Converse.
AREA NO. 10: All or parts of West Feliciana Parish.
South of Como Bayou from Old L & A railroad tram to Mississippi River, east of Mississippi River to Thompson's Creek, west of Thompson's Creek to the Old L & A railroad tram, west of L & A Railroad tram to Como Bayou.
AREA NO. 11: All or parts of East Feliciana, East Baton Rouge and St. Helena Parishes.
West of La. Hwy. 43 from Mississippi line to junction of La. Hwy. 16, north of La. Hwy. 16 from La. Hwy. 43 to Amite River at Dennis Mills, west of Amite River from Dennis Mills to Stony Point; north of Stony Point—Burch Road from Stony Point to Fred; and east of La. Hwy. 67 from Fred to Mississippi line.
AREA NO. 12: All or parts of Washington and St. Tammany Parishes.
East of La. Hwy. 450 from the Mississippi State line to La. Hwy. 10, south of La. Hwy. 10 from La. Hwy. 450 to Tchefuncte River, east of the Tchefuncte River from La. Hwy. 10 to Lake Pontchartrain, north of Lake Pontchartrain from Tchefuncte River to the Mississippi line.
5 days with or without dogs:
November 25—November 29, 1966.
AREA NO. 13: All or parts of East Baton Rouge, St. Helena, Livingston and Ascension Parishes.
South of La. Hwy. 16 from Montpelier to the Amite River at Dennis Mills, east of the Amite River from Dennis Mills to Stony Point, south of Stony Point—Burch road from Stony Point to Fred, east of La. Hwy. 67 from Fred to U. S. Hwy. 61, north and east of U. S. Hwy. 61 from the junction of La. Hwy. 67 to La. Hwy. 42, north of La. Hwy. 42 from U. S. Hwy. 61 to La. Hwy. 447 at Port Vincent, west of La. Hwy. 447 from

Port Vincent to U. S. Hwy. 190 at Walker, north of U. S. Hwy. 190 from Walker to La. Hwy. 441 at Holden, west of La. Hwy. 441 from Holden to Montpelier.
24 days with or without dogs:
November 25—December 4; December 26—January 8, 1967—plus
15 days still hunt only: December 10—December 24, 1966.
AREA NO. 14: All or parts of Caddo, Webster, Claiborne, DeSoto, Red River, Union, Bienville, Jackson, Winn, Lincoln, Sabine, Natchitoches and Bossier Parishes.
West of U. S. Hwy. 167 from Arkansas line to Joneshoro, north of La. Hwy. 4 from Jonesboro to Dugdemona Creek to La. Hwy. 126, north of La. Hwy. 126 to La. Hwy. 9, east of La. Hwy. 9 from La. Hwy. 126 to La. Hwy. 155, north of La. Hwy. 155 to Mill to Readhimer to Saline to Ashland to Black Lake Bayou, west of Black Lake to La. Hwy. 9, north of La. Hwy. 9 from Black Lake to intersection U. S. Hwy. 71 and La. Hwy. 84, east and north of U. S. Hwy. 71 and La. Hwy. 84 from junction of La. Hwy. 9 to Coushatta, north of La. Hwy. 84 from Coushatta to Armstead, west of La. Hwy. 1 from Armstead to Lake End, north of La. Hwy. 174 from Lake End to Converse, east of U. S. Hwy. 171 from Converse to Mansfield, north of U. S. Hwy. 84 from Mansfield to Logansport to the Texas line except Barksdale Air Force Base which shall be open for either sex still hunting only for 20 days, Dec. 2-11; Dec. 30-Jan. 8, 1967 and EXCEPT that portion of Caddo Parish south of U. S. Hwy. 80 from Shreveport to Greenwood, east of La. Hwy. 169 from U. S. Hwy. 80 to Spring Ridge, east of La. Hwy. 789 from Spring Ridge to Keatchie Bayou, north of Keatchie Bayou, Wallace Lake and Bayou Pierre to La. Hwy. 175, north of La. Hwy. 175 from Bayou Pierre to La. Hwy. 1, west of La. Hwy. 1 from La. Hwy. 175 to U. S. Hwy. 80, which shall be closed and EXCEPT that portion of Bossier Parish west of La. Hwy. 3 from Bossier City to Benton to La. Hwy. 160 at Hughes, south of La. Hwy. 160 from Hughes to Red River, east of Red River to Bossier City which shall be closed.
24 days still hunting only, no dogs:
November 25—December 4;
December 26—January 8, 1967.
AREA NO. 15: All or parts of portions of St. John the Baptist Parish.
That portion of St. John Parish south of Pass Manchac from Lake Pontchartrain to U. S. Hwy. 51, east of U. S. Hwy. 51, from Pass Manchac to La. Hwy. 638 (Frenier Beach Road) north of La. Hwy. 638 from U. S. Hwy. 51 to Lake Pontchartrain, west of the shore of Lake Pontchartrain from La. Hwy. 638 to Pass Manchac.
17 Days Still Hunting Only:
November 25-December 10, 1966.
AREA No. 16: Natchitoches, Vernon, Beauregard, Calcasieu, Jefferson Davis, Allen, Rapides and Avoyelles Parishes.
East of La. Hwys. 6, 1 and 119 from Red River to Gorum, south of Gorum, Mink, Kisatchie Road (La. Hwy. 118) to La. Hwy. 117, east of La. Hwy. 117 from Kisatchie to Leesville, south of La. Hwy. 8 from Leesville to the Texas Line, east of the Texas Line to Anacoco Bayou, north and east of La. Hwy. 111 to U.S. Hwy. 190, north of U.S. Hwy.

190 from La. Hwy. 111 to DeRidder, east of La. Hwy. 27 from DeRidder to Sulphur, north of U.S. Hwy. 90 from Sulphur to the intersection, La. Hwy. 27 and U.S. Hwy. 90 between Lake Charles and Iowa, north and east of La. Hwy. 27 and 14 through Holmwood and Hayes to La. Hwy. 99, west of La. Hwy. 99 to U.S. Hwy. 90 at Welch, south of U. S. Hwy. 90 from Welch to the junction of U. S. Hwy. 165 at Iowa, west of U. S. Hwy. 165 from Iowa to Kinder, south and west of U. S. Hwy. 190 from Kinder to Ragley to La. Hwy. 112, north and west of La. Hwy. 112, 113, and 112 from U. S. Hwy. 190 to Sugartown to Pitkin to Union Hill to Hineston, west and north of La. Hwy. 28 from Hineston to U.S. Hwy. 71 at Alexandria, east of U.S. Hwy. 71 from Alexandria to Bunkie, north and west of La. Hwy. 115 from Bunkie to Big Creek, south of Big Creek from La. Hwy. 115 to the Rapides-Avoyelles Parish Line, east of the Rapides-Avoyelles Parish line from Big Creek to Red River, west of Red River, from Rapides-Avoyelles Parish line to La. Hwy. 6.

5 Days Still Hunting Only: November 25-November 29, 1966 AREA No. 17: Cameron Parish South and east of Mermentau River from the Gulf of Mexico to Grand Lake, south of Grand Lake, Callicon Lake and Old Intracoastal Canal to the Cameron-Vermilion Parish line, west of Cameron-Vermilion Parish line from the Old Intracoastal Canal to the Gulf of Mexico, first day (Nov. 25) to be open to the taking of either sex deer.

1966-67 GAME MANAGEMENT AREAS SCHEDULE

For all Game Management Areas, except as otherwise specified: DEER: 5 days of deer hunting unless otherwise specified: November 25-November 29, 1966 either sex until the designated number of deer are taken, after which the remaining days of the total 5 days, if any, shall be open to "bucks only" hunting. Notification of type hunt to be made when daily permit obtained.

PERMITS: When daily permits are required these may be obtained at the permit stations located on or near the Game Management Areas.

Season permits, where required, may be obtained in advance beginning September 1 from any Commission District Office; P. O. Box 915, Minden; P. O. Box 4004, Ouachita Station, Monroe; P. O. Box 278, Tioga; P. O. Box 426, Ferriday; P. O. Box 405, De-Ridder; P. O. Box 585, Opelousas; P. O. Box 14526, Southeast Station, Baton Rouge; 400 Royal Street, New Orleans. Turkey Season permits obtained at District Offices listed above beginning March 1, 1967.

JACKSON-BIENVILLE:
Deer: 350 Any Deer and 5 days, November 25-29, Daily Permit. Bucks only 7 days, December 26-January 2, Season Permit.
Squirrel & Rabbit: October 1-31, Season Permit.
Quail: December 31-February 28, 1967, Season Permit.
BODCAU:
Deer: Same as outside except still hunt; Season Permit. All Small Game: Same as outside but still hunt only; Season Permit.
Dogs allowed only for bird hunting. No permanent duck blinds. No quail hunting on Foreign Game Bird Experimental Area, Marked Area.

SODA LAKE:
Waterfowl hunting permitted Monday, Wednesday and Saturday mornings only (until 12 noon) throughout waterfowl season, to include experimental teal season, Season Permit.

Small game seasons open during statewide season EXCEPT no hunting allowed during the closed portions of waterfowl seasons. No permanent duck blinds.
CANEY (Middle Fork & Corney):
Deer: Same as outside EXCEPT still hunt only: Season Permit. All Small Game: Same as outside but still hunt only; Season Permit.
Dogs allowed only for bird hunting. No permanent duck blinds.
UNION:
Deer: 100 Any Deer and 5 days: November 25-29, Daily Permit. Bucks only, 7 days, December 26-January 1, 1967, Season Permit.
Squirrel & Rabbit: October 1-31, Season Permit.
Quail: December 31-February 28, 1967, Season Permit.
RUSSELL SAGE:
Deer: Same as outside with Season Permit EXCEPT first Day (November 25) - Any Deer with Daily Permit.
All Small Game: Same as outside but Still Hunt Only.
GEORGIA-PACIFIC:
Deer: 5 Days, November 25-29, first day any deer; remainder; Bucks only; Daily Permit.
Quail: December 24-January 1, 1967, Season Permit.
Turkey: April 1-3, one-half day, mornings only, Daily Permit.
Squirrel & Rabbit: October 1-23, Season Permit, No Dogs.
EVANGELINE:
Deer: 100 Any Deer and 5 Day, November 25-29, Daily Permit.
Squirrel & Rabbit: October 1-31, Season Permit.
Quail: December 31-February 28, 1967. Season Permit.
CATAHOULA:
Deer: 350 Any Deer and 5 Days, November 25-29, Daily Permit.
Squirrel & Rabbit: October 1-31; Season Permit.
Quail: December 31-February 28, 1967. Season Permit.
FORT POLK:
Deer: 300 Any Deer and 3 Days: November 25-27, Daily Permit. Legal bucks only: Concurrent with adjacent areas. Season Permit.
All Small Game: All Statewide season applicable, Season Permit. The use of dogs prohibited during deer seasons.
*Military clearance required in addition to Season Permit - check locally.
SABINE:
Deer: 75 Any Deer and 5 days; November 25-29; Daily Permit.
Squirrel & Rabbit: October 1-31; Season Permit.
Quail: December 31-February 28; Season Permit.
LUTCHER-MOORE:
Deer: Same as outside with Season Permit, Still Hunt Only, Bucks Only. All Small Game: All statewide seasons applicable, the use of dogs permitted for quail hunting only; No quail hunting during deer season; Season Permit.
RED DIRT:
Deer: 300 Any Deer and 5 Days; November 25-29; Daily Permit.
Squirrel & Rabbit: October 1-31; Season Permit.
Quail: December 31-February 28, 1967; Season Permit.

ALEXANDER STATE FOREST:
Deer: 80 Any Deer and 5 Days; November 25-29; Daily Permit.
Squirrel & Rabbit: October 1-31; Season Permit, Check locally for restricted areas.
CALDWELL:
Deer: 150 Any Deer and 5 Days; November 25-29; Daily Permit. Bucks only, 7 Days; December 26-January 1, 1967; Season Permit.
Squirrel & Rabbit: October 1-31; Season Permit.
Waterfowl: Same as Outside Season, EXCEPT no waterfowl hunting during deer season and no permanent duck blinds, Season Permit.
SALINE:
Deer: Bucks Only 5 Days, November 25-29, Daily Permit.
Squirrel & Rabbit: October 1-November 20; Season Permit.
Waterfowl: Same as outside season, EXCEPT no waterfowl hunting during deer season and no permanent duck blinds, Season Permit.
CONCORDIA:
Squirrel & Rabbit: October 1-November 20; Season Permit.
All other seasons closed for development work on Area.
WEST BAY:
Deer: 5 Days; First day either sex hunting till 12:00 noon, remaining 4 days full day hunting for Bucks only, November 25-29; Daily Permit.
Squirrel & Rabbit: October 1-31; Season Permit.
Quail: December 31-February 28, 1967. Season Permit.
Turkey: April 1-2, Gobblers Only, Daily Permit.
THISTLETHWAITE:
Deer: 5 Days; First Day any Deer, remaining 4 Days Bucks Only, November 25-29 (Hogs may be killed during Deer Season); Daily Permit.
Squirrels & Rabbits: October 1-16 and November 5-13, mornings only till 12:00 noon; Still Hunt Only, Daily Permit.
CITIES SERVICE:
Deer: Same as Outside, Still Hunt Only, Season Permit.
Quail: January 9-February 28, 1967, Season Permit.
All Small Game (Except Quail) same as outside, Still Hunting Only; Season Permit.
ZEMURRAY PARK:
Deer: December 5, 6, and 7, Any Deer; 200 Hunters per day.
Non-transferable permits are to be issued by mail in advance of hunts. Louisiana resident hunters only to be selected at public drawing in Baton Rouge on Tuesday, November 15. Applicants do not have to be present Post card applications must be made by United States mail only, to Fish and Game Division, Louisiana Wild Life and Fisheries Commission; Capitol Station, Baton Rouge, Louisiana, being postmarked between Thursday, October 13 and Saturday, November 12 and received at the above address no later than Monday, November 14. Hunter's failure to include big game license number will void his application. Only one application will be considered. State choice with one (1) alternate date for one (1) of three designated days. No more than two names per application will automatically void such application.
Duplicate applications by any hunter will cancel all his applications. No small game hunting permitted.
Archery: Hunting of Deer with bow and arrow permitted each Saturday and Sunday (weekends) beginning October 8 ending November 20, 1966 Daily Permit.

23

WILDLIFE-O-GRAM

WILD DUCK POPULATION SHOWS INCREASE

The Department of the Interior said today that North America's duck breeding population has made a remarkable comeback from the low period of 1965 and that the increase, plus improved nesting conditions on the vital northern prairie breeding grounds, is expected to produce a larger flight of ducks this fall.

John S. Gottschalk, Director of the Department's Bureau of Sport Fisheries and Wildlife, said that aerial surveys by the Bureau's flyway biologists which revealed the increase in breeding ducks also showed that water levels in the prairie potholes and sloughs have held up well during the summer months.

GARTNER HEADS OWAA AGAIN

John Gartner, editor of "Western Outdoors," has been re-elected as president of the Outdoor Writers Association of America. At its 1966 annual meeting at Port St. Lucie, Florida, the OWAA continued the entire slate of officers to serve in the coming year.

Vice presidents are Homer Circle, feature editor for "Sports Afield," Hurley Campbell, editor, "Southern Outdoors Magazine," and Bob Munger, Nebraska free lance writer and photographer. Seth L. Myers, outdoor editor for the "Sharon (Pennsylvania) Herald," continues as OWAA secretary and treasurer.

COMMISSION PHOTOGRAPHER WINS AWARD

Robert N. Dennie, chief photographer for the Wild Life and Fisheries Commission, won the outstanding photographic award at the 1966 OWAA convention. The award consisted of a boat, motor and trailer.

WATER POLLUTION CONTROL BILL BEGINS TO MOVE

Efforts to amend and strengthen the Federal Water Pollution Control Act begin to show promise of success before Congress adjourns because of recent Senate and House actions, according to the Wildlife Management Institute. Ordered favorably reported by the Senate Committee on Public Works is a revised version of S.2947 by Senator Edmund S. Muskie (Maine) and nearly 50 others.

HARMON ELECTED SECRETARY-TREASURER OF AACI

Steve Harmon, chief of the education and publicity division of the Louisiana Wild Life and Fisheries Commission, was elected secretary-treasurer of the American Association for Conservation Information at the international organization's 25th annual conference held in Hot Springs, Arkansas this month.

The AACI is an association of conservation information specialists from 44 states and five Canadian provinces, dedicated to the advancement and improvement of conservation information programs throughout the North American continent.

The 1967 conference will be held in British Columbia with the 1968 meeting scheduled for New Orleans.

Cloyse Bond of the Oklahoma Wildlife Conservation Department was elected president of the association; Jim Sherman of the Iowa Conservation Commission, first vice-president and William Dillinger of the California Department of Fish and Game Commission, second vice-president.

The *B*ird of the month

GROUND DOVE
Columbigallina passerina

Charles R. Shaw

THIS minute member of the pigeon family is not much larger than the common House (English) Sparrow. A plump little grayish brown bird, with a short square blackish appearing tail, the common name of Ground Dove is self explanatory since this is obviously a small dove and it spends most of its time on the ground where the constant nodding of its tiny head as it walks along is a noticeable diagnostic characteristic. Several other colloquial names have been applied to it, including Mourning Dove and Moaning Dove from the soft cooing call, as well as Little Dove and along the eastern seaboard sometimes Tobacco Dove.

In flight the short rounded dark tail and the conspicuous bright rufous flash of the wing patches make its identification fairly certain to those who have had any training or experience in the identification of song birds. It is doubtful, however, if many of the sportsmen of our state of Louisiana, where we had a harvest of over one million Mourning Doves during the last year, are aware of the presence of this small relative of their favorite upland game bird. This in spite of the fact that it is not actually a rare species as far as records go although it probably passes unnoticed far more times than it is recognized. It has been recorded during all months of the year and throughout the state at least as far north as Monroe. I personally have seen these birds on several occasions and as far north as Grant Parish.

Although most often seen in pairs, (some authorities think they may mate for life) they may gather into small flocks, particularly in the fall and winter.

These are breeding birds in our state, since several nests have been reported from the southwestern portion of the state where the occurrence of the Ground Dove can be considered locally common although certainly not uniformly widespread.

Considering the life history of this bird over its entire range (which includes the Southeastern and Gulf Coast states and down into Mexico) it has a very long nesting period, ranging from February through October. In this respect, of course, as in many others, it is similar to its larger cousin, the Mourning Dove.

The nest is a rather flimsy structure of grass, twigs, straw, etc., usually on the ground but sometimes in bushes, rarely placed very high, however. The usual clutch is two white eggs as is true of most of its near relatives. However, as is often the case where such a small number of eggs is laid there may be two, three or even four broods raised during the long nesting season. Thus the total number of young is geared to compensate for normal natural mortality factors and thereby hold the population level at the normal carrying capacity of the habitat. The young birds, which are somewhat lighter colored than their parents, are fed by regurgitation, presumably in the same fashion as other members of the pigeon family.

The food of the adults consists primarily of grass and weed seeds. Cultivated areas, beaches, overgrazed pastures and similar areas with at least some bare ground seem essential for normal feeding and the birds do not prefer areas with too heavy or thick cover.

Although classed with the game birds there is no open season on this little dove and it is under the protection of both state and federal laws. ✳

RETURN REQUESTED
Louisiana Wild Life and Fisheries Commission
400 Royal Street
New Orleans, Louisiana 70130

WATERWAYS SAFETY IS A NEVER ENDING ASSIGNMENT FOR THE

Enforcement Agent

Louisiana is laced with rivers, lakes, bayous and other flowing streams and boating has become one of the state's most popular outdoor recreation sports. Enforcement agents of the Louisiana Wild Life and Fisheries Commission are kept busy all during the year in an effort to keep boating and water accidents to a minimum. These agents go about their work in a calm, courteous but firm manner. Checking boaters to see if they have approved life jackets is routine for these men dedicated to the cause of conservation and the safety of our outdoorsmen. (Photo by Robert N. Dennie)